Date Night Conversations

Recapture the Magic with Great Couple's Communication Tools

By Thomas E King

For information about permissions to reproduce selections from this book
write to TEK publishing
3820 Cleveland Avenue North, Suite 400
Arden Hills, MN 55112

Legal Notice

CONTENTS

Introduction

The purpose of this book is to provide you with guidance on how to talk about the key topics every couple should discuss. Do you have regular date nights with your partner? If, so, congratulations because you are taking steps to strengthen your marriage or relationship that other couples may think about but not actually accomplish. On your dates, do you sometimes wonder what you should talk about or find yourself avoiding talking about things you know you should discuss? Many times couples keep conversations pretty superficial and as a result they fail to deepen their relationship.

This book will, first of all, help you identify the important topics that can strengthen your relationship, and secondly, provide you with the structure to have the right kind of discussions on each topic. You may find you need to jump into some topics right away and that is fine, but I believe it is best to work through each conversation in the order they are presented.

I have been married for over 35 years and have worked with couples for about 25 years and I have studied and read dozens of books on the subject of relationship health. Consequently what you will find here represents many points of view including my own. I have tried to sift through much of the information available and give you what I think are the key topics that can make or break your relationship. I have made a good faith effort to identify the authors and other sources of information contained here and to recommend other things to read if you want to explore any particular topic further.

Special tribute goes to my wife who has been my faithful partner and companion in our journey through life. She has taught me so much about life, about love, and about myself. We have laughed, cried, shouted, struggled, played, loved, and literally grown up together and I am eternally grateful for our time as partners. Our story, like yours, represents the power of marriage to make us better people. I hope these conversations help you grow as individuals and as a couple into your full potential. I also hope you take what you need, what works for you, and have fun learning together.

One more note before getting into the book. This was originally written to be a companion book to an online course I designed called Reimagine Marriage: The Heart of Work-Life Balance. If you are curious and want more information on any of these topics you can access that course at http://www.reimaginemarriage.com/study-course/

Thank you for purchasing this book. Please REVIEW this book on Amazon. I need your feedback to make the next version even better. Thank you so much!

Chapter 1
CAN WE TALK ABOUT OUR RELATIONSHIP STORY?

What is the story you tell yourself about your relationship and your partner? When couples have difficulties they often create a story to explain what is going on. Most often, in that story the other person is responsible for the problems. You know how it goes:

- If only she would stop doing that everything would be fine
- If only he would do more of this then I would be happy
- I would – fill in the blank- if he would – fill in the blank

This is called projection and you fail to recognize your own issues being reflected back to you in your partner. You are being triggered by your partner, but what is being triggered are areas of sensitivity within yourself, areas that you do not yet see clearly and have not resolved. In order to break through your roadblocks each person must assume responsibility for his or her own growth and be willing to look in the mirror. These conversations, starting with conversations with yourself will help you do just that.

You see, the stories you have told yourself about your marriage and about your partner have colored your perception of reality. What is even more seductive is that whenever you hold something to be true, you will naturally find evidence to support your point of view. So step one in resolving problems in your relationship is to suspend judgment and be open to seeing what is really going on.

To help couples understand these dynamics more clearly I created the ***Dynamic Marriage Map***. This is a four quadrant framework which describes the interaction of two dynamic forces that determine the quality of every marriage or significant relationship. One of these forces is the level of optimism and connection you feel towards one another. This is influenced by your relationship skills or your capability to be emotionally intimate. The other force is the level of development or differentiation that each individual brings into the relationship. Your level of personal development is influenced by how well you worked through your life conditioning and the places where you are emotionally stuck. This reflects your own capacity to be a mature and loving person.

Take some time now to study the framework and see if you can recognize yourself and your relationship. Notice that the story you have been telling yourself is related to the quadrant you are in and that this story will change as you move through the stages. If you are paying close attention you will also begin to see the themes of your own developmental issues in your story.

Optimism/Connection Level
Capability to Love

Promise/Idealism
•Hope to get my core needs met
•Desire to be known
•Desire to make partner happy
•Resolve unfinished business

Possibilities/Fulfillment
•Interdependence
•Co-commitment to the wholeness of each other
•High intimacy
•Spiritual connection/meaning

Peril/Disillusionment
•Don't get needs met
•Don't feel understood
•Feel inadequate
•Default defenses and sensitivities
•Withhold love and energy

Parallel/Independence
•Personal growth is focus
•More emotional and spiritual awareness as individual
•Get fulfillment outside of marriage
•Low intimacy

Development/Consciousness Level

Capacity to Love   © Grow it Forward, LLC 2009

Understanding the Map

Almost all couples start out in quadrant one, Promise/Idealism. It is easy to feel infatuated in the early stages of marriage or your relationship and you can't seem to get enough of each other. The story you start out with usually is very idealistic and you see your partner as someone you have always been looking for. This stage of love feels great but it is not sustainable. It feels like two people sitting in a canoe trying to paddle towards one another, which is fun at first but you don't get anywhere. Sooner or later you need to focus on getting on with other things in life and when you do one or the other starts to feel upset.

In quadrant two, Peril/Disillusionment, the issues you are not fully aware of and have not resolved show up. The things you found endearing in Q one are now the things that drive you crazy. His silent strength is now a wall he hides behind. Her bubbly personality is now flighty or demanding. Couples often feel angry and disillusioned in this stage and begin to blame one another. Now it feels like two people sitting in a canoe, back to back, trying to paddle away from each other. Of course, this is very unsatisfying so most people try from time to time to get back into Q one where it felt better. However, without resolving the real issues, couples find themselves circling between Q one and Q two.

When you get tired of spending so much negative energy in your relationship you may find yourself resolving the tension by focusing on other things. In quadrant three,

Parallel/Independence, you turn your attention to your career, your children, your hobbies, or whatever comes along at the expense of intimacy. You grow individually in many ways but you also grow apart if you are not building your relationship skills and deepening your connections. Soon it starts to feel like you are not even in the same canoe anymore.

Some couples find their way to quadrant four, Possibilities/Fulfillment, and when they do they find the deep satisfaction of being in a loving relationship in which each person has worked on their own personal development and nurtured deep connections and commitment to one another. Now you are comfortable with yourself and can enjoy times of intense closeness and passion and times of being apart for the purpose of individual exploration. Couples in this stage have a vision of what they are creating and operate like true partners. Finally it feels like understanding how to steer your canoe through whatever comes as a team.

For more detailed explanation of this model go to **www.dynamicmarriagemap.com**

Conversation questions:

1.   Where do you each think you are now on the map?

2.   Have you been at different stages at different times?

3.   What stories have you been telling yourself about your partner and your relationship?

4.   Are you willing to open your mind to changing your story and work your way into quadrant four?

Chapter 2
CAN WE TALK ABOUT WHAT IS GOOD IN OUR MARRIAGE?

Key Principles

- People do not need to be fixed, they need to be accepted and affirmed
- If you want someone to get better, build him or her up rather than tearing him or her down
- Love and honor are the only rules you need
- Language creates reality
- What you focus on grows
- Negative language and focus keeps people in a negative mindset
- Positive language and focus creates a possibility mindset

Often times when couples have been stuck in a struggle, patterns of negativity, or lack of connection, they forget why they got together in the first place. It can be very helpful to stop and remember and reflect on what those qualities are that you saw in one another. It is also helpful to name the things you do like about your partner and your relationship. As noted above, what you focus on grows stronger so don't spend all your energy focusing on what annoys you or what you want to change about your partner. Spend some time talking about what is good, what is working, what you love about each other, and what you want to build on. In this chapter you will find three worksheets or sets of questions. Don't try to get through them all in one sitting but use them to provoke a series of self-reflections and conversations.

Exercise 1

Reflection questions:
Describe a high point experience in your marriage, a time when you were most alive and engaged.

Without being modest, what is it that you most value about yourself, and your contribution to marriage?

What is it you most value about your partner and his/her contribution to the marriage?

What are the core factors that give life to your marriage, without which the marriage would cease to exist?

Exercise 2

Imagine you have awakened from a long, deep sleep and your marriage is as you always dreamed it would be. Your ideal state has become reality. What do you see? What is going on? How have things changed? How does it feel?

Exercise 3

What three wishes do you have to enhance the health and vitality of your marriage?

1.

2

3.

Exercise 4

Using this information and the ideas from the exercises above, create a story together of your vision for your marriage. Be creative and have fun with this. For example, you may want to write a narrative story or a play, build a vision board using pictures and symbols, or make a mind movie (put your pictures and images into a video, using music or whatever captures your story).

Chapter 3
CAN WE TALK ABOUT KEY DECISIONS AFFECTING OUR LIVES?

This chapter is focused on understanding your personal history and key decisions that have influenced how you live your life. Why is this important for your marriage? It's important because you bring the effects of your experiences and history into your relationships. Many times decisions made in your youth, conscious or not, are still at work in your life. Once you begin to examine your own history you will be able to see themes that run throughout your story and patterns that you keep repeating.

My suggestion is that you work on the following exercises individually first and then share and discuss your insights and observations with one another. It is important to not judge yourself or your partner in any of this, but just allow the information to emerge freely. Sometimes memories can be painful so please be compassionate with yourself and each other. If you become overwhelmed you may want to seek the help of a professional. Feel free to contact me if you have any questions or concerns.

Exercise 1

Write your autobiography

1. Think about your life in 5 year increments: 0-5, 6-10, 11-15 Etc.

2. Record whatever memories come up, both positive and negative

3. Think of your life as a story. What themes or patterns do you see?

4. If you were writing a book of your life, what would the title be?

Key Decisions

Some of the content in the following exercises was adapted from **Relationship Breakthrough: How to Create Outstanding Relationships in Every Area of Your Life** by Cloe Madanes

What are key decisions?

When life is difficult during childhood we make some judgments about the reasons for those difficulties and the meaning of them. Due to lack of life experience and the natural self-centeredness of childhood, we often assume that somehow we are causing the troubles in our life and that this is the way life is. So, for example, if we have an abusive or neglectful parent, we conclude we are doing something wrong, somehow we must deserve it, or for some reason we are not loveable. As an adult we can see most of these types of conclusions are immature and false, but as a kid we believe them and internalize them.

In order to cope with the difficulties we face as a child and the judgments we make about them, we make some choices or decisions about how to manage life. Many times these are unconscious decisions or at least decisions we don't remember as an adult. Some of them become key decisions that determine how we engage with some aspect of life and we carry it forward into adulthood. These key decisions are about how to protect ourselves, how to cope, and how to compensate for what we experience and what we feel. There is a positive intent behind these decisions and in their original context serve a purpose, but in the context of adulthood they become self-limiting and dysfunctional.

Key decisions often take the form of rigid and absolute beliefs. Here are some examples you may recognize:
- It is not safe to trust people in authority
- It is not safe to let anyone get too close or really know me
- I must try to please key people in my life in order to be loved
- I must be the best or achieve high marks in order to be acceptable
- Life is unpredictable so I must control as much as possible
- People don't like me if I say what I think or feel so I will keep quiet

How to identify key decisions

First, look at your current circumstances because they are a reflection of your beliefs and assumptions. If you find there is a pattern to your circumstances and your behavior then you know you made a key decision that is being played and re-played out in your life. For example, if you go from one bad relationship to another, you likely made a key decision about yourself and relationships that keeps you from experiencing loving, intimate connections. Or if you have chronic problems with money, again there is a key decision about what money means or what you deserve. Maybe you find yourself exhausted because you are always working and never give yourself a break. Did you make a decision at some point that you must constantly strive to do more, have more, be more?

Next, if you haven't completed your autobiography, take some time to review your life story. Think back over your life and write down your memories about what you experienced, what life was like, what you felt. Start as far back as you can. What do you remember between the ages of 0-5, 5-10, 10-15, and so on?

After you have a good collection of memories written down, take some time to look for significant events and for themes.
- What patterns can you see?
- How did you respond to difficult events or pattern of events?
- How did you try to make yourself feel better?
- What did you do to try to succeed, get attention, or feel significant?
- Can you see ways you learned to protect yourself?
- By answering these questions and reflecting on the themes in your life you should be able to see some key decisions you made that have influenced the course of your life and how you have lived. Now use this insight to complete the process below.

Exercise 2

Seven Steps to Understand and Change Key Decisions

Step one:
Go back through your autobiography and reflect on your childhood. Think about these questions:
- What kind of relationship did you have with your parents?
- What experiences had a profound impact on you?
- What did you learn from these experiences?
- How did you cope when things were difficult?

Step two:

Identify key decisions you think you made. Think about these questions:

- What key decision or decisions did you make, consciously or not? For example, you may have decided it is not safe to trust anyone so you decided to only really trust yourself. Or you may have decided that the only way you matter is if you are achieving something and you therefore strive to always be the top of the class.
- When did you make your key decision?
- Why did you make it?

Step three:

Connect to the consequences of the Key Decision. Every decision carries consequences beyond the immediate situation and may affect other decisions and other people in your life. Think about these questions:

- How does or did the key decision serve you? Any time you repeat a behavior, it is because you are gaining something from it.
- What does it accomplish?
- What are the side effects or unintended consequences?

Step four:

Commit to change. If a key decision is not serving you well then you can decide that enough is enough. An obsolete decision no longer needs to keep you from loving and living to your fullest. Think about these questions:

- What key decision am I ready to change?
- What more useful decision can I make now?
- What do I think will happen if I let go of an old key decision?

Step five:

Build up emotional resources. Changing habitual ways of thinking and behaving can be difficult so be patient and persistent. It takes more than insight to change habits. You must also teach your emotional self that it is okay to change and you learn emotionally through experiences. Here are some ways to build up your ability to develop new habits:

- Do one small thing that contradicts the key decision from the past. Do something that is opposite of how you normally react.
- Emphasize the ways you have succeeded in life. Don't dwell on guilt or regret.
- Recognize how the key decision has served you as well as held you back.
- When you made your key decision, what other alternatives did you give up?
- What adjustments can you make that maintain the benefits but also allow you to experience the things you have sacrificed?

Step six:

Strategize ways to reclaim your identity. Sometimes when you make a key decision you give up or disconnect from a part of yourself. Now you can make a plan to be a more authentic version of yourself. For example:

- If you long ago decided you need to be quiet and compliant, you may now decide you want to be strong and decisive.
- If you decided long ago to never show your feelings, you may now decide it is okay to sometimes share your sadness and fear.
- Think about ways you can reclaim long-lost possibilities you sacrificed in order to be accepted
- You are not your experiences, your thoughts, or your feelings. There is an authentic you inside who is separate from these things.
- Step into the place of the authentic self who observes all these things. Notice yourself becoming aware of yourself.

Step seven:

Take specific action and visualize the benefits.

You can decide when, where, and how you want to change your thoughts, feelings, and habits. Reinforce your efforts by visualizing the benefits of being your authentic self. Here are examples of actions you may take:

- Apologize for the way your key decision has hurt others.
- Mentally rehearse your new decision and new way of being.
- If you have trouble understanding what you feel, use your physiology to find your emotion. What can you do physically to find your emotion? For example, stand up straight, pull your shoulders back and feel powerful.
- Ask for support and feedback from your partner and other people you trust.
- Practice new behaviors until they feel normal.

Recognize that your partner may not understand or be comfortable with the changes you are making. It is important to be respectful of your partner's concern but don't let it discourage you. Use your date night conversations to talk about what you are learning about yourself, what you are trying to change and why. Most likely your partner will support positive change once he or she understands. When you ask for feedback, listen carefully and apply what makes sense. Change is often clumsy, like learning to play a new instrument, but with practice you will get better. As you become more authentic you will become more interesting and generally happier.

My Key Decision

I have personally identified and worked on several key decisions in my life. One example stems from an event when I was about 12 years old. My father had a heart attack and was taken to the hospital. I was too young to visit, according to hospital rules at the time, and I remember being afraid I would never see my dad again. Well it turns out my father recovered and lived a full life but I was forever impacted by that event. I remember fairly consciously deciding that I never want that to happen to me.

As a result of that key decision I became very health conscious at an early age. I studied the causes of heart disease and learned the vocabulary of cholesterol, saturated fats, etc. I started restricting my diet and exercising more. I also was very aware of my father's behaviors and tried to influence him to be healthier.

There were positive and negative consequences to my key decision. On the positive side I developed some good health habits that have continued into adulthood. On the negative side I became far too anxious about my health at a young age. I denied myself some of the pleasures of indulging in junk food with my peers once in a while and was just more rigid than I needed to be. Another negative side effect showed up in my marriage as I tried to educate my wife on what and how to eat and stay fit. Needless to say, this was not generally appreciated.

I have learned over time to modify this decision and the behavior that goes with it. I am less anxious about my health and have given myself permission to eat french fries once in a while. I have made a conscious effort to be less annoying to my wife and friends about their health habits. I am still health conscious and take good care of myself but have found a much more comfortable balance. Change has been gradual and anxiety can still get triggered but now I know what is going on and can consciously choose my response. Perfection is not required.

Exercise 3

The One Big Thing

What is the one thing about yourself, that if you could change it, improve it, or master it, then it would make a huge difference in the quality of your life and your marriage?

To answer this question, get input and feedback from others. Start with your spouse, and then ask trusted friends who know you well and maybe even ask your kids. Listen carefully to their feedback and accept it graciously and gratefully. They are trying to help you improve, so for heaven's sake do not argue or disagree with their feedback. Just say thank you.

You may get several things suggested to you so you will need to look for themes, sift the information and then decide what your one big thing is. Now go to work on it.

Chapter 4

CAN WE TALK ABOUT CORE NEEDS AND THE LANGUAGE OF LOVE?

A number of scholars and authors have written about our primary human needs. Perhaps the most well-known is Abraham Maslow who wrote about the hierarchy of needs:

1. Biological and Physiological needs - air, food, drink, shelter, warmth, sex, sleep.

2. Safety needs - protection from elements, security, order, law, limits, and stability.

3. Belongingness and Love needs - work group, family, affection, relationships.

4. Esteem needs - self-esteem, achievement, mastery, independence, status, dominance, prestige, managerial responsibility.

5. Self-Actualization needs - realizing personal potential, self-fulfillment, seeking personal growth and peak experiences.

Another related framework that I find useful is described by Chloe Madanes in her book **Relationship Breakthrough**. This framework of core needs has also been used by Anthony Robbins in his teaching and coaching. According to Madanes, the premise of human needs psychology is that each individual is a self-determined entity able to make choices about how to get his or her needs met. Biology, chemistry, and early life experiences are all influences that we can choose or refuse to be effected by.

We turn to the important relationships in life to meet our needs and the needs of our significant others. If you understand your partner's core needs as well as your own you can do a better job of meeting them. Core needs are like secret levers. If you know what your loved one needs and values most and how he or she satisfies those needs, then you'll understand how to satisfy him or her.

Love languages is another framework made popular by Gary Chapman in his book **The 5 Love Languages: The Secret to Love that Lasts**. The basic premise is that what feels like love and caring behavior to me may not communicate love and caring to you. We all have a variety of love languages but we need to understand our differences and preferences and use that knowledge to effectively communicate love to one another.

Exercise 1

Core Psychological Needs
Adapted from **Relationship Breakthrough** by Chloe Madanes

Definitions:

Certainty: The need for predictability, security, and safety.

Variety: The need for change, adventure, playfulness, and stimulation

Significance: The need to feel important, valued, and respected

Love and Connection: The need for emotional bonding and intimacy

Growth: The need to develop, learn, advance, and evolve

Contribution: The need to make a difference, have a purpose, and leave a legacy

Rank order which needs are most important to least important to you.

Certainty: _____

Variety: _____

Significance: _____

Love and Connection: _____

Growth: _____

Contribution: _____

Using a scale from 1-10, 1 = very little and 10 = the highest possible, rate how well you feel your needs are being met in your relationship or situation.

Certainty: _____

Variety: _____

Significance: _____

Love and Connection: _____

Growth: _____

Contribution: _____

Self-Awareness Questions

When a core need is not being met or is being threatened, what kind of emotions do you notice within?

How does your body react?

What kind of thoughts do you notice in your mind?

What do you see yourself doing to defend yourself or to get your need met?

What reactions do you notice when your core needs are being met sufficiently?

How can you get your needs met or addressed in a healthier way?

How can you do a better job of meeting your partner's core needs?

Exercise 2

Love Languages
Adapted from **The 5 Love Languages** by Gary Chapman

Read the following list of love languages individually. Which are the top two ways you prefer to receive love?

Words of Affirmation:
- I like the way you……
- Thanks for…..
- I love you more than anything
- Compliments
- Words of encouragement
- Spoken kindness

Quality time:
- Give undivided attention
- Quality conversations – listen to understand, not to give advice
- Quality activities

Receiving gifts:
- Symbols that he or she was thinking of me
- Need not be expensive gifts
- Consider giving a parade of gifts

Acts of service:
- Do things you know your spouse wants you to do
- Please by serving your spouse
- Must be done with a positive spirit
- Ask your spouse what he or she would like you to do

Physical touch:
- Holding hands, kissing, hugging, sex
- Find out how your spouse wants to be touched
- Sexual desire may be separate from the emotional need for love

After you have each determined your love languages discuss them with one another.

- Do you find yourself giving love in the language you would like to receive it?

- Ask your partner for examples of how to communicate more effectively in his or her love language.

- Make a commitment to use love languages to demonstrate love to one another consistently.

Pay attention and discuss the implications of this information. Each person must take responsibility for him or herself but it is also a way to show love to your partner. For example, if the husband's top love language is quality time and the wife's love language is words of affirmation, then a day hanging out doing a fun activity will make him quite happy. This experience may be just okay for her however, unless the husband remembers to tell her how much fun it was hanging out with her and how much he appreciates her. Then both partners will feel affirmed by the experience.

Exercise 3

Couples Questionnaire

Please complete the following questions individually in as much detail as possible. You may want to create a bullet point list of the things that come to mind or write out a paragraph. Share your answers with each other when you are ready.

1.   I like it when my partner _____.

2.   I wish my partner would_____.

3.   It makes me feel safe when my partner_____.

4.   I feel cared about when my partner_____.

5.   I feel respected when my partner_____

6.   My partner likes it when I _____.

7.   My partner wishes I would _____.

8.   My partner feels safe when I_____.

9.   My partner feels cared about when I_____.

10. My partner feels respected when I _____

Chapter 5
CAN WE TALK ABOUT SEX AND INTIMACY?

Sex and intimacy, desire and love are surprisingly difficult for many couples to manage. And yet, it is not at all surprising when you think about all the conditioning we have around sexuality and the vulnerability that is required for intimacy. Add to that the challenge of trying to keep the flames of passion going with one person over time and you end up with some interesting paradoxes.

Intimacy is created through sharing yourself with one you love. There are many expressions of intimacy and we all have different levels of awareness and willingness to share who we are. Some, maybe most of us have lost sight of the light and the beauty within and it feels as if we never really knew ourselves at all. How can we reveal what we do not know?

I do not think, as one often hears, that we cannot love someone until we fully love ourselves or that we cannot create intimacy without fully knowing ourselves. It is in honestly coming together with another admitting we don't fully know and love ourselves that helps to reveal our essence. Saying "I don't know" is a place of honesty, humility, and vulnerability that allows learning to take place. Through such transparency we can help one another grow and mature. We shape and influence one another for better or worse.

In her book, **Mating in Captivity: Reconciling the Erotic and the Domestic**, Esther Perel eloquently describes another such paradox:

Love enjoys knowing everything about you; desire needs mystery. Love likes to shrink the distance that exists between me and you, while desire is energized by it. If intimacy grows through repetition and familiarity, eroticism is numbed by repetition. It thrives on the mysterious, the novel, the unexpected. Love is about having; desire is about wanting. An expression of longing, desire requires ongoing elusiveness. It is less concerned with where it has already been than passionate about where it can still go. But too often, as couples settle into the comforts of love, they cease to fan the flame of desire. They forget that fire needs air.

So keeping passion alive in a long term relationship requires being intentional about creating the conditions in which love and intimacy are nurtured on the one hand, and sex and desire are given air to breathe on the other. As described in the Dynamic Marriage Map, this means continuing your individual journey of becoming who you are, and also building skills to deepen connections with each other. It means not putting the burden on sex to make you feel validated, but giving freedom for sex to express love, passion, playfulness, or deep connection.

It means revealing yourself to your partner and yet keeping some mystery about you. It means realizing that you do not belong to each other; rather each must take ownership of self. As soon as you are able to acknowledge that your separateness and mystery are always present, sustained erotic desire becomes a real possibility.

Exercise 1

This very short exercise was adapted from **Mating in Captivity** by Esther Perel:

Take a deep breath and hold it in as long as you can. Notice that at first the fresh oxygen feels great but then as it turns to carbon dioxide and you need to let it out and take another breath. You can't choose between inhaling and exhaling; you have to do both. It is the same with intimacy and passion; both must be cultivated in your relationship.

Exercise 2

Hugging Until Relaxed Exercise
Adapted from **Passionate Marriage** by David Schnarch
The goal of this exercise is to practice holding unto yourself while holding onto your partner. This means staying connected with yourself, being aware of your thoughts and feelings, quieting or calming yourself while also being connected to your partner. This exercise shows how well you can relax and keep your balance even if your partner "loses it".
Instructions:

- Face your partner and stand on your own two feet
- Put your arms around your partner and embrace each other
- Hold the hug longer than normal and as long as you both want to and until you feel relaxed
- Focus on yourself and notice what you feel
- Use your reactions to hugging to work on yourself rather than each other
- Quiet yourself down – way down
- Scan your body for tension and relax it.
- Talk to yourself mentally in a calm and soothing way
- Deepen and slow your breathing
- Be aware of self and other – be present

Discussion questions and thoughts

This exercise can help you see your level of differentiation. Differentiation refers to your level of emotional maturity and ability for interdependence. It is your ability to stand on your own two feet, physically and emotionally, when you are close to others. It allows you to stay close while your partner is bouncing off the wall.

- Share with each other what your experience was during this exercise.

- On a scale from 1-10, how difficult was it to feel completely relaxed? Why?

When you draw your sense of stability from your partner, you have to try to control him or her at all times. In short, you can never relax.

- Did your partner hold on too tightly or not tight enough?   Too long or not long enough?

In contrast, when your sense of stability comes from yourself you can just let your partner go, focus on yourself, calm yourself down, and then reach out from a place of stability. It's not about becoming more heartless or hard-hearted – it's taking better care of your own heart.

- How well are you able to feel your own heart?

Well-differentiated couples hold onto each other and try to make one another feel good. The difference is the outreach is a choice rather than a necessity. It is done for the other person rather than one's own needs.

- Can you tell the difference between your needs and your partner's needs? Try to put them into words.

If you won't let go of your partner and let her struggle to stand on her own, she doesn't have to confront herself, she just has to confront you. You will never know if she really wants connection with you because you do all the wanting for both of you.

- Do you find it hard to let your partner struggle to solve his or her own problems and find his or her balance? How does this show up in your behavior?

If you want to help your partner, hold onto yourself and quiet yourself down. If you want to soothe your partner, give him or her someone to hold who's already quiet.

- Practice this skill often, for yourself and for your partner.

Exercise 3

Personal Sex Guidelines

Answer the following questions and then use them as a conversation starter with your partner.

1. I find sex most satisfying when……

2. It helps me get in the mood for sex when…..

3. What excites me the most during sex is….

4. It turns me off when….

5. I feel closest to you when…..

6. When making love the most important thing is….

7. When one of us doesn't feel like making love I would like us to …..

8. What I appreciate the most about you sexually is…….

9. What I like about myself sexually is……

10. I wish we could……

Chapter 6
CAN WE TALK ABOUT CONFLICT AND PROBLEM SOLVING?

Conflict within relationships can be destructive or constructive. It can cause you to spiral down into hurtful cycles or prompt you to spiral up into personal growth. Whether you spiral up or down depends on how you interpret and respond to what happens between you. Many of the exercises and conversations you have worked on through this book will help you deal more effectively with differences that come up. This chapter will help you find better strategies to live, love, and work together so you can solve problems instead of just re-cycling them.

Most of us spiral into conflict when we get emotionally triggered. This happens when something is said or done that is hurtful or misunderstood. It is natural to be disturbed and defensive if you feel hurt. If, however, you find yourself overreacting to a situation then there is also something historical going on. This particular situation, whether it is a behavior, a word, tone of voice, or even a look has reminded you of something that upset you in the past. When that happens you tend to project blame onto your partner for making you feel upset and you do what you have learned to do in the past; maybe lash out, withdraw, or break down. Your over-reaction will be confusing and threatening to your partner who will likely react negatively, which simply confirms your thoughts that he or she is totally at fault. You are flooded with emotions from the past and it feels like whatever happened is happening all over again. Now you have two people showing up with their childhood emotional selves trying to deal with an adult problem. If you have been together for a while you may repeat the same themes over and over and you find yourself saying things like "you always do this to me!"

Clearly there must be a better way to deal with problems. It begins with understanding the above dynamics of a negative cycle and putting a stop to it. You must recognize when you are triggered, own your feelings as yours, and then step back and observe yourself and what is happening. Then you can consciously let go of your initial upset and the need to blame your partner. When you do that your conflict and upset feelings can be seen as opportunities to let go of blocked energy from the past and help each other heal and grow. Even if your partner did something stupid, you will be able to deal with it much better if you bring your adult, conscious self forward to address it. Then and only then can conflict lead to constructive conversations and problem solving.

Exercise 1

Co-committed Problem Solving Process

This exercise is adapted from **Conscious Loving: The Journey to Co-Commitment**
By Dr. Gay Hendricks and Dr. Kathlyn Hendricks

Reflect on the following questions when you are dealing with a conflict. Use these as a guide to resolve issues together.

1. What am I feeling?
    o   Face each other and tell the truth about your feelings.
    o   Use feeling words, not mental explanations. For example, "I feel like you are wrong" is a thought, not a feeling. "I am hurt or furious" is a feeling.
    o   Where in your body do you feel it? What physical sensations?
    o   Remember feelings come in layers. For example, what is underneath your anger? Do you notice hurt? How about fear?

2. What do I want?
    o   Think about the outcome you really desire or the need you want to have fulfilled.
    o   Make positive requests about what you want. For example, "I want you to pick an activity for us to do once in a while."
    o   Avoid complaints or talking about what you don't want.

3. How is my past coloring my present?
    o   Overreactions tend to be historical. Look at your sensitivities and overreactions.
    o   What is familiar about what you are feeling?
    o   Do you see patterns or themes?
    o   What patterns of behavior do you see in your relationship?
    o   Example: "My father always said I was his dumbest kid. When you don't want to spend time with me I feel like you don't think I'm good enough."
    o   Take this opportunity to forgive and let go of negative energy from your past.

4   .   What am I getting out of staying stuck?
  o   Negative behavior often has a pay-off, whether or not you are aware of it.
  o   Old patterns are comfortable even if painful. There is often anxiety about changing patterns or behavior.
  o   What is this conflict preventing you from doing or seeing?
  o   Learn to see your issues as allies, waiting to help you break through.

5.   What do I need to say?
  o   Even if you know what you should say, most of us are programed to withhold the truth for fear of the other's reaction.
  o   Face each other and tell the truth in a spirit of love, without punishing one another for it.
  o   Examples: "Sometimes I wish we had never gotten married or had kids." "I don't like our elaborate lifestyle." "I don't like going shopping with you."

6.   What agreements have I broken?
  o   Is there something you have not confessed?
  o   How might this issue be creating a barrier between you?
  o   Can you support each other in dealing with the whole truth? (exercise 2 deals with this in more detail)
  o   How can I be of service to you?
  o   How can I help you reach your goals?
  o   How can we be co-creators of our future?
  o   Focus on building positive energy for each other.

Exercise 2

Forgiveness and Resolving Relationship Traumas

Adapted from **Hold Me Tight: Seven Conversations for a Lifetime of Love**
by Dr. Sue Johnson

If there is an issue that has caused a trauma or serious hurt in your relationship, such as infidelity or financial irresponsibility, then do not ignore it or try to bury it.

Unresolved traumas do not heal. Time does not heal all. Injuries to one another must be honestly confronted and resolved to the best of your ability. Sometimes people decide they must leave their relationship in order to move forward. Even if that is what you decide it is still important to forgive in order to heal. If you decide to stay together then it is critical to work towards forgiveness and restore trust in one another. Many couples need help working through serious breaches of trust so please do not be afraid to see a therapist if you are stuck. The process outlined below is meant to guide your thinking as you talk about concerns.

Forgiveness process

1. The injured partner must describe the pain
    o   Do not assume your partner knows exactly how you feel or see the situation
    o   Describe the specific situation you are upset about
    o   What is the meaning of what happened from your perspective?
    o   How does it affect your sense of safety and trust?
    o   State your thoughts and feelings about it

2. The partner who caused the pain must stand in the storm
    o   Allow the injured partner to express the depth of his/her feelings
    o   Acknowledge your partner's feelings and pain
    o   Listen to understand, not to defend or justify yourself
    o   Acknowledge your part in the situation

3.   Take accountability
- o   As the partner who caused the pain, you must take ownership of how you hurt the other person
- o   Show how you are impacted by your partner's pain
- o   Express remorse, regret, and sincere apology

4.   Address needs
- o   The injured partner identifies what he/she needs to bring closure
- o   Seek clarity of what will help
- o   The injuring partner needs to affirm and attempt to meet the requests
- o   Change behaviors, especially those that are causing hurt

5.   Forgiveness is a process
- o   Repeat steps 1-4 as often as necessary
- o   Agree to take small steps forward
- o   Make and keep commitments, over and over
- o   The injured partner needs to decide to forgive and accept the apologies
- o   Remember, if an issue from your past is being triggered by this event, you need to be willing to let it go in order to move forward. Go back and review the Co-Committed Problem Solving Process.

6.   Create a new story
- o   Things can never be the same
- o   Your relationship must be re-defined going forward
- o   Create a new quality of relationship together
- o   Integrate recovery into your story of renewal and deeper connection

Exercise 3
Competing Commitments

Adapted from **Immunity to Change,** by Kegan and Lahey

If you find yourself stuck or continuously undermining your own progress then you may need to do some reflection to identify and neutralize any hidden agenda or competing commitments. Use the table below to help you think this through. You may need the perspective of a friend, spouse, or a professional to help you see yourself accurately.

Goals or desired behaviors	Behaviors that undermine my goal. What do I do or not do that stops me?	Invisible competing commitments I may have? For example, did I make a commitment to never back down from a fight? Go back and review your key decisions.	Core belief that supports this competing commitment. What big assumption am I making? What is the positive intent?

Action steps

If you have identified a competing commitment bring it out into the light and give it a voice. This may be an internal dialogue or it may help to write it down as a conversation. Ask yourself:

- Is this belief or assumption 100% true?

- What is the fear connected to this competing commitment?

- What is the purpose of keeping this commitment alive?

- Is there a way to honor this commitment directly and reduce the fear?

- How can you change your belief so that it is more accurate for you today?

- Will you release your fear or move forward through your fear?

- Can you create an If-Then plan for this competing commitment?
   o   If this behavior or fear shows up….
   o   Then I will….

Remember to be persistent. Success depends on taking the right actions consistently over time. The key is to let go of whatever does not serve you well in the present. If it is important enough to you to resolve your issues then never give up!

Chapter 7
CAN WE TALK ABOUT COMMITMENTS TO LOVE FOR A LIFETIME?

Have you been having meaningful conversations with your partner? Have you noticed growth, breakthroughs, or more connection? If you have started to feel some positive momentum that is wonderful but how do you keep it going? One suggestion is to keep this book handy and make it a part of your relationship going forward. Perhaps you can use it as a tool when you are feeling stuck. Perhaps you want to make a ritual of picking out one or two chapters to discuss every year on your anniversary.

Keeping positive energy flowing between you requires commitment to the well-being of your selves and your relationship. You can decide right now to be done with brokenness and embrace wholeness. Consciously decide to let go of all the dysfunction in your life. It is not you and it does not have to define you or your relationships. Your authentic self is whole, peaceful, and joyful. Remember this, focus on this, and live your life from that place of identity. You can create the conditions in your marriage that support this awareness of wholeness of each of you. I invite you to take in the following commitments and make them your own. May you be blessed with love for a lifetime!

Ten Commitments

Commitment 1: I commit to loving and honoring myself and my partner as much as I am able.

Commitment 2: I commit to claiming responsibility for creating my life. I take 100% responsibility for me. There will be no blaming and there are no victims.

Commitment 3: I commit myself to my own developmental journey as an individual.

Commitment 4: I commit myself to support the full development and growth of my partner.

Commitment 5: I commit to understanding and revealing my most important needs.

Commitment 6: I commit to understanding and responding with love to my partner's most important needs.

Commitment 7: I commit to speaking the truth as I know it in a spirit of love.

Commitment 8: I commit to keeping my agreements and I consciously choose to be trustworthy.

Commitment 9: I commit to practicing forgiveness and compassion towards myself and my partner.

Commitment 10: I commit to cultivating closeness and intimacy in my marriage and allowing space for each of us to grow as individuals.

Additional Resources by the Author

http://www.reimaginemarriage.com

- Home study course - Re-imagine Marriage: The Heart of Work-Life Balance
- Pre-marital home study course
- Free blog articles
- Couples counseling and coaching

http://www.growitforward.com

- Individual counseling
- Executive coaching
- Couples coaching
- Free blog articles

http://emerging-leadership.com

- Leadership development programs
- Executive coaching

References and Recommended Reading

Chapman, Gary. The 5 Love Languages: The Secret to Love that Lasts. Chicago: Northfield Publishing, 2010.

Hendricks, Gay, and Kathlyn Hendricks. Conscious Loving: The Journey to Co-Commitment. New York: Bantom Books, 1992.

Johnson, Sue. Hold Me Tight: Seven Conversations for a Lifetime of Love. New York: Hachette Book Group, 2008.

Kegan, Robert, and Lisa Laskow Lahey. Immunity to Change: How to Unlock the Potential in Yourself and Your Organization. Boston: Harvard Business School Press, 2009.

Madanes, Cloe. Relationship Breakthrough: How to Create Outstanding Relationships in Every Area of Your Life. New York: Rodale inc., 2009.

Maslow, A.H. A Theory of Human Motivation. Psychological Review, 50, 370-396. 1943

Perel, Esther. Mating in Captivity: Reconciling the Erotic + the Domestic. New York: HarperCollins, 2006.

Schnarch, David. Passionate Marriage: Keeping Love & Intimacy Alive in Committed Relationships. New York: W. W. Norton & Company, 2009.

About the Author

Thomas King, MSW, M.Ed., LICSW is a therapist in private practice in Arden Hills, MN. He works with couples and adults to help them become the best of who they are. He is a partner/owner of Emerging Leaders Association, LLC, which is dedicated to executive coaching and leadership development. He has worked in healthcare, government, major corporations, and an international consulting firm, providing counseling, coaching, consulting and training services. He lives in St. Paul with his wife and is the proud father of two daughters who are married and they each have two daughters and one more on the way.

Tom is available as a therapist, coach, workshop leader, retreat facilitator, and speaker.

Contact information

tom@growitforward.com

tom@emerging-leadership.com

Linked In: http://goo.gl/bpkO4

Facebook: http://goo.gl/wFkXJ

Twitter: http://goo.gl/vDlZD

Made in the USA
Lexington, KY
04 August 2015